W9-CLK-933

Flower Drum Song

A Musical Play

Music by RICHARD RODGERS
Lyrics by OSCAR HAMMERSTEIN, 2nd
Book by OSCAR HAMMERSTEIN, 2nd and
JOSEPH FIELDS

Based on the Novel by C. Y. LEE

FARRAR, STRAUS AND CUDAHY
NEW YORK

CAST OF CHARACTERS

In Order of Appearance
Original Cast, December 1, 1958,
St. James Theatre

Madam Liang	*Juanita Hall*
Liu Ma	*Rose Quong*
Wang San	*Patrick Adiarte*
Wang Ta	*Ed Kenney*
Wang Chi-Yang	*Keye Luke*
Sammy Fong	*Larry Blyden*
Dr. Li	*Conrad Yama*
Mei Li	*Miyoshi Umeki*
Linda Low	*Pat Suzuki*
Mr. Lung (The tailor)	*Harry Shaw Lowe*
Mr. Huan (The banker)	*Jon Lee*
Helen Chao	*Arabella Hong*
Professor Cheng	*Peter Chan*
Frankie Wing	*Jack Soo*
Head Waiter	*George Young*
Night Club Singer	*Anita Ellis*
Dr. Lu Fong	*Chao Li*
Madam Fong	*Eileen Nakamura*

SYNOPSIS OF SCENES

ACT ONE

ACT TWO

Flower Drum Song

Act I

ACT ONE

Scene 1

The living room in the house of Master Wang Chi-Yang.

SCENE: *The house is architecturally Victorian with Chinese decoration superimposed. It represents the blending of San Francisco and Hong Kong which permeates the story. The chairs are high and straight-backed. The lamps, the miniature garden on a low table, the god of Longevity, dominating the room from one wall—all assert the oriental spirit on an occidental background.*

    A large, broad window and a door to the street fill out the back wall. Off Left one goes to the kitchen, off Right to the rooms upstairs.

AT RISE: MADAM LIANG *at telephone.* LIU MA *stands near her with a list in her hand.* WANG SAN *sits in armchair eating an apple.*

MADAM LIANG
(Into phone)
Hello . . . Is this the Ping Wah Super Market? This is Madam Liang. I would like to place my order. How is your octopus today? Oh . . . No, never mind. Then send me two pounds of sea horse, one pound of dried snake meat and a box of longevity noodles.
(To LIU MA*)*
Anything else?

9

LIU MA

(*Indicating list*)
Thousand Year Eggs.

MADAM LIANG

Oh, yes—
(*Into phone*)
And a dozen thousand year eggs. Thank you, Mr. Sung.
(SHE *hangs up.* LIU MA *turns and exits, Right*)

TA

(*Entering from Left*)
What is my little brother doing home from school?

SAN

They sent me home. I got in a fight.

MADAM LIANG

He fights, and all Chinatown will think he is a descendant
of a low bred family. I don't know what I will say to your
father.

TA

Isn't Father home?

MADAM LIANG

No, my nephew. He has gone to the bank to have his hundred
dollar bill changed.

TA

I need my allowance.

SAN

Have you got a date, Ta?

TA

As a matter of fact, I am going out with Johnny Lee and two young ladies.

SAN

A couple of tomatoes!

MADAM LIANG

Foreigners?

TA

No, Chinese girls.

SAN

Chinese tomatoes!

MADAM LIANG

What is her family name?

TA

Low. I met her on a blind date.

MADAM LIANG

Blind date?

TA

That is when a friend arranges for you to meet a young lady whom you don't know. Miss Low has a Thunderbird.

SAN

Big deal!

MADAM LIANG

Go to your room, and remember—any more fighting and I will take you out of that school.

SAN

If I stay in that school, I better join Blue Cross!
(SAN *exits, Left*)

TA

(*Looking at his watch*)
My aunt, do you think you can lend me ten dollars? I will
pay you after Father pays me.
(MADAM LIANG *gives* TA *the money*)

TA

Thank you, Aunt Liang.

MADAM LIANG

(*probing*)
I heard you talking to yourself in your room last night. Were
you memorizing your speech?

TA

No. I was memorizing a Chinese poem.

MADAM LIANG

To recite to Madam Thunderbird?

TA

There is one poem I think might appeal to her.

MADAM LIANG

What poem?

TA

It starts: "Along the Hwang Ho Valley . . ."

MADAM LIANG

Ah yes, I remember. . . .
　(*Singing:*)
　　Along the Hwang Ho Valley,
　　Where young men walk and dream—

TA

　　A flower boat with singing girls
　　Came drifting down the stream.

TA

　　I saw the face of only one
　　Come drifting down the stream . . .

　　You are beautiful,
　　Small and shy,
　　You are the girl whose eyes met mine
　　Just as your boat sailed by.
　(MADAM LIANG *nods her head as if she knows it well*)
　　This I know of you,
　　Nothing more.
　　You are the girl whose eyes met mine
　　Passing the river shore.
　　You are the girl whose laugh I heard,
　　Silver and soft and bright,
　　Soft as the fall of lotus leaves
　　Brushing the air of night.
　　While your flower boat
　　Sailed away,
　　Gently your eyes looked back on mine,
　　Clearly you heard me say:
　　"You are the girl I will love some day."
　(TA *has sung the last line with great feeling.* MADAM
　LIANG *studies him as he speaks. The music of a second
　refrain continues under the dialogue.*)

TA

Similar things happen to me when I am at a football game and see a face in another row of the grandstand, or sometimes when a girl goes by in a car—our eyes meet for an instant.

MADAM LIANG

My nephew, do you sleep well at night?

TA

No. Not lately.

MADAM LIANG

Thinking of girls does not induce sleep.

TA

You do not know how a girl can trouble a man, especially at night.

MADAM LIANG

Yes, I do. I used to be one. . . . and I troubled a man until he became your uncle. He used to read poetry to me. . . .
(TA *comes up behind his aunt, puts his hands on her shoulders affectionately, and sings to her:*)
   You are the girl whose laugh I heard,
   Silver and soft and bright,
   Soft as the fall of lotus leaves
   Brushing the air of night.
(MADAM LIANG *joins*)
   While your flower boat
   Sailed away
   Gently your eyes looked back on mine,
   Clearly you heard me say:
   "You are the girl I will love some day."

LIU MA

(*Entering with bowl and putting it on table*)
Ginseng Soup!
(SHE *exits immediately*)

MADAM LIANG

I hope it does not get cold.

TA

I must go, Aunt Liang. Tell my father—
(HIS *speech is interrupted by the sudden opening of the front door.* WANG CHI-YANG *comes in, slams the door behind him and dashes into the room greatly agitated. A man of sixty, with a kind face despite a drooping gray mustache which gives him a stern look. He is dressed in a loose gown of blue satin and traditional black satin trousers. He places his hand over his heart and sucks in a deep breath.*)

MADAM LIANG

(*Greatly alarmed*)
What is it, my sister's husband?

WANG

I have been robbed! The hundred dollars I changed are gone.

TA

Where were you robbed?

WANG

Right in front of the house next door! (TA *runs up to the door, opens it and looks out*) A bandit poked something hard against my back. I quickly raised my hands. He snatched my money and fled.

TA

(*Coming back into the room*)
Here, my father, take some Ginseng soup. You'll get another coughing spell.

(HE *hands his father the bowl of soup and sits him down.*)

(WANG *takes the soup*)

MADAM LIANG

I am glad you were robbed! How many times have I told you, you should keep your money in a bank?

WANG

It has always been safe under my bed.

MADAM LIANG

Your bedroom may be safe for everything else, but not money.

WANG

I want you to report this to the American government. I want two soldiers to guard my house day and night.

TA

Father, you cannot order the American government to guard your house.

MADAM LIANG

You are not a Feudal Lord—this is not China!

WANG

For five years you have been going to that American Citizenship School, and all you have learned is—

(*Imitating her voice*)
"This is not China!"

MADAM LIANG

(*Showing off her knowledge*)

The American government has three departments: Judicial, Legislative and Executive. All that a citizen who has been robbed can do is ask the Police Department of the Executive Department to catch the thief—

TA

(*Interrupting her*)

Please!

(*Turning to his father*)

What did he look like?

WANG

Don't ask me what he looked like. All white men look alike.

TA

Father, why don't you put your money in a bank?

WANG

Money is like a man's wife, strangers should not get their hands on it.

TA

May I go? I'm late for my appointment.

(WANG *nods*)

Good-bye, Father—good-bye, my aunt.

MADAM LIANG

(*Pointedly*)

I hope you enjoy your blind date.

(TA *makes a warning gesture to her as if to say "don't tell father," and exits. But* SHE *wants to tell father*)

Blind dates are girls one doesn't know!

WANG

My son must not court girls he does not know. His wife must be born in a suitable month, from a house with a high door.

MADAM LIANG

My teacher in the Citizenship School says to bring a wife from China under the immigration quota takes ten years. By that time Ta will be thirty-one and you will be seventy.

WANG

And I might never see a grandchild!

(DOORBELL *rings.* MADAM LIANG *opens it admitting* SAMMY FONG. *He is a good-looking Americanized Chinese in his thirties. He is a politico and a fixer.*)

MADAM LIANG

Sammy Fong!

SAMMY

The one and only me. How've you been Madam Liang?

MADAM LIANG

Not good, not bad.

SAMMY

And how's the old Master?

WANG

(*Coldly*)

Mr. Fong, why am I being honored with your visit?

SAMMY

Let me lay it on the line. Madam Liang told me you were in the market for a bride for your son.

WANG

According to my boy's horoscope, unless he finds a bride from the East, his marriage will not be a happy one.

SAMMY

A bride from the East is a hot commodity today.

MADAM LIANG

There are immigration laws—

SAMMY

For the average citizen, yes. But not for Sammy Fong. In my book there's only one law—supply and demand. You want the eight-ball in the side pocket? You got it!

WANG

You have an unfortunate way of expressing yourself.

SAMMY

I went to a progressive school. When I got out, my mother sent for a Hong Kong picture bride as a graduation present.

WANG

What has this to do with us?

SAMMY

A good question! This kid arrived in town today and I can't handle her.

WANG

Why not?

SAMMY

You're not going to believe this, but she's too good for me. She's a fine, filial, obedient girl. That's not for me. A dame's got to beat my brains out, or I couldn't be happy with her.

WANG

How do you know?

SAMMY

I've tried it both ways. For five years I've been slugging it out with the sweetest kid on the West Coast.

WANG

As one of the Elders of the Family Association, I can tell you now your contract must be honored. You must marry your picture bride!

SAMMY

That's why I've come to you. It takes ten years to get one of those girls over here. I'm offering you mine for immediate delivery. You could have a grandchild by April!

MADAM LIANG

You hear that, my sister's husband?

SAMMY

Your son could step in, I could step out, and the bride would save face. And believe me, that little face is worth saving. She's got skin like white jade, and she's built like a Ming vase. She'd be the daughter-in-law of the year!

WANG

Her family—is she from a house with a high door?

SAMMY

You could ride through it on a camel without knocking your hat off!

WANG

(Reflectively)
How old is this picture bride?

SAMMY

She's a sweet nineteen, born in the year of the rabbit!

MADAM LIANG

Ta was born in the year of the sheep. They would go well together.

SAMMY

Like vodka and tonic!

WANG

I would like to have this young woman meet me.

SAMMY

That's what I figured. So I brought her along. She's waiting outside.
(SAMMY FONG hurries off)

WANG

(Indignantly, to MADAM LIANG)
How could you discuss our family problems with a man who runs a fan tan game and a night club?

MADAM LIANG

The Fongs are members of our Family Association, and I play canasta with his mother!

(SAMMY FONG *returns with* DR. LI, *a man in his late fif-*
ties. He is poorly dressed, but carries himself with dig-
nity. MEI LI *follows him in. She wears a pigtail. Her*
pretty face is glowing with health. She carries their lug-
gage bound with ropes.)

SAMMY

This is Dr. Li and his daughter, Mei Li—Master Wang Chi-
Yang and his good sister-in-law, Madam Liang.

WANG

You honor my house, Dr. Li.

DR. LI

Your distinguished name has been rumbling in my ears like
thunder.

MEI LI

(*Crosses to* WANG)
Ten thousand benedictions, Sir, —and to you, Madam.
(MEI LI *executes three kowtows*)

SAMMY FONG

(*"Selling"* MEI LI)
You don't get them like that over here any more!

WANG

Come here, let me look at you, my child.
(MEI LI *goes over to* WANG *obediently.* WANG *holds her*
chin. She opens her mouth. He looks at her teeth, then
passes his eyes down to her small feet.)
I see no outside blemishes.

SAMMY FONG

Right off the assembly line—not a scratch on her!
(*Handing contract to* WANG)
Here's your contract. It's a pleasure to do business with you,
Master Wang. So long Dr. Li. So long Mei Li.

MEI LI

So long too Sammy Fong!
(SAMMY *gives her a long, wistful look*)

SAMMY FONG

Oh, if I only knew what was good for me!
(*As* SAMMY *starts off,* DR. LI *calls.*)

DR. LI

Mr. Fong!
(SAMMY *comes down to him.* DR. LI *has a deep firmness
in his voice*)
My daughter is still *your* picture bride, and if your plan does
not please us, we shall address ourselves to the Three Family
Association!

SAMMY FONG

(*Worried*)
No, don't do that. They'll only louse it up, and once they make
a decision, you're a dead duck.

DR. LI

(*Bewildered*)
A dead duck?

SAMMY FONG

(*Making a getaway*)
Don't worry—we'll get together—we'll kick it around.
(HE *waves to* MADAM LIANG *and exits*)

23

WANG

Dr. Li, sit down, rest yourself. You must be weary.
(DR. LI *bows and sits.* WANG *resumes his appraisal of* MEI LI)
She has a good chin. The blessing of longevity.

DR. LI

She is as strong as a cow, and just as amiable.

MEI LI

Thank you, my father.

DR. LI

And when she eats regularly, she is inclined to be plump.

WANG

A sign of fertility.

MADAM LIANG

(*Sympathetically*)
You have not been eating regularly?

DR. LI

By the time we got to Formosa, our money was given away in bribes. Our next problem was to get to Manila.

MADAM LIANG

(*Again showing off her learning*)
That is in the Philippine Islands. The United States, in its treaty with Spain in 1901—

WANG

Enough! (*To* DR. LI) And how did you make your way from Manila?

24

DR. LI

On a tramp steamer bound for Vancouver.

MEI LI

When the ship docked we ran away.

WANG

Why?

DR. LI

We had no papers.

MADAM LIANG

You came in illegally?

DR. LI

To come in under the quota would take another five years.

MEI LI

In five years I will be twenty-four. That is too old to get married.

WANG

How did you get here from Vancouver?

DR. LI

When we found little settlements we gave a show.

MEI LI

With the Flower Drum.

WANG

You can sing Flower Drum Songs?

DR. LI

Yes. Get them my daughter. Get the drum and the gong.
(MEI LI *runs up, opens a suitcase and takes out a flower*
drum and a gong)

WANG

It's been a long time since I heard a Flower Drum Song.

MADAM LIANG

(*Calling off Right excitedly*)
Liu Ma! Liu Ma—come!

DR. LI

(*Taking the gong from* MEI LI)
Please make room!
(HE *beats his gong and addresses them as if they were a*
street crowd)
Kind-hearted and distinguished friends! My daughter and I
are going to give a show—a Flower Drum Show from the
North! Songs of filial piety, songs of loyal officials—

WANG

Songs of ghosts!

MADAM LIANG

Songs of love!

WANG

And songs of—

WANG, MADAM LIANG and DR. LI

Misery.
(DR. LI *beats the gong once more and* LIU MA *enters from*
Right)

26

DR. LI

Ah! A venerable lady has come! Now we have a crowd, we can start. Kind-hearted and distinguished friends: If the song is good—

MEI LI

Give me a little applause when I am through.

DR. LI

If her song is bad—

MEI LI

Give me applause, too.
(SHE *sings:*)
> My father says
> That children keep growing,
> Rivers keep flowing, too.
> My father says
> He doesn't know why
> But, somehow or other, they do.

DR. LI

> They do!
> Somehow or other, they do.

MEI LI

(*Beating her drum in accompaniment*)
> A hundred million miracles,
> A hundred million miracles
> Are happening every day.
> And those who say they don't agree,
> Are those who do not hear or see.
> A hundred million miracles,

A hundred million miracles
Are happening
Every Day!

DR. LI

Miracle of . . . Changing Weather.

MEI LI

When a dark blue curtain
Is pinned by the stars,
Pinned by the stars to the sky,
Every flower and tree
Is a treat to see,
The air is very clean and dry.
Then a wind comes blowing
The pins all away.
Night is confused and upset!
The sky falls down
Like a clumsy clown—
The flowers and the trees get wet.

ALL

Very wet!

A hundred million miracles,
A hundred million miracles
Are happening every day.

MEI LI

And when the wind shall turn his face,
The pins are put right back in place!

ALL

A hundred million miracles
A hundred million miracles

Are happening
Every
Day!

MADAM LIANG

In every single minute
So much is going on
Along The Yellow River or The Tiber or The Don.

ALL

A hundred million miracles!

WANG

A swallow in Tasmania
Is sitting on her eggs,
And suddenly those eggs have wings and eyes and
    beaks and legs!

ALL

A hundred million miracles!

MADAM LIANG

A little girl in Chungking,
Just thirty inches tall,
Decides that she will try to walk and nearly doesn't
    fall!

ALL

A hundred million miracles!
(*Increasing in volume*)
    A hundred million miracles,
    A hundred million miracles,
    A hundred million miracles
    Are happening every day!

FLOWER DRUM SONG

MEI LI

(*Very softly*)
> A hundred million miracles,
> A hundred million miracles
> Are happening every day.
> My father says
> The sun will keep rising
> Over the eastern hill.
> My father says
> He doesn't know why,
> But somehow or other it will.

ALL

> It will!
(*Harmonizing softly*)
> Somehow or other it will. . . .
(*There is a moment of silence.*)

MADAM LIANG

(*Putting her arm around* MEI LI, *as if accepting her into the family*)
Come, my child, I will show you to your room.
> (SHE *starts to lead* MEI LI *off.* WANG *and* DR. LI *remain onstage in a warm handshake as the lights fade.*)

END OF SCENE ONE

ACT ONE

Scene 2

A hill overlooking San Francisco Bay.

SCENE: *On the drop the Golden Gate Bridge can be seen through the usual fog. This is revealed as the walls of Scene 1 slide off into the wings. Simultaneously the various parts of this set slide on, tall trees on either side, a bench downstage, backed by a lilac bush and a lamp-post.*

AT RISE: TA *and* LINDA *are silhouetted against the drop, hand in hand. As the scene is set and the lights come up, they walk downstage.*

LINDA *is a thoroughly Americanized Chinese girl.*

TA

I wonder why Johnny and Anna stayed in the car. Maybe they thought we wanted to be alone.

LINDA

I do . . . don't we?

TA

(With false jauntiness)
You bet.

LINDA

That is why fellows and girls come up here.

TA

Would your brother approve?

LINDA

(*Uncertainly*)
My brother?

TA

The other night you told me he was an officer on an ocean liner.

LINDA

Oh—my *brother!* He's at sea most of the time. He's very strict with me. He doesn't like me to go out with boys, at all.

TA

He sounds almost as bad as a jealous lover.

LINDA

(*Looking at* TA *half suspiciously because he has hit the nail on the head so accurately*)
Yeah.
(*Then* SHE *rattles on quickly.*)
He's been taking care of me for a long time. He buys my clothes, pays for my apartment. He even bought me the Thunderbird. You know—to save carfare. He pays for my singing lessons—

TA

Are you serious about a singing career?

LINDA

Not particularly.

TA

What is your ambition? What do you want to be?

LINDA

I want to be a success as a girl. Oh, it's nice to have outside accomplishments like singing, cooking or first aid. But the main thing is for a woman to be successful in her gender.

TA

But don't you think it's important to do one thing very well?

LINDA

Sure—that's what I mean.

 (LINDA *sidles up to* TA *and looks up at him provocatively*)

It's getting kind of chilly up here.

TA

Want to go?

LINDA

 (*Moving closer to him*)

No—but I think I need something around me.

TA

 (*Rising*)

I'll get your sweater. It's in the car.

 (LINDA *looks after him as if he were something she's never met with before. Then she turns back and sings contemplatively*)

33

LINDA

I'm a girl and by me that's only great!
I am proud that my silhouette is curvy,
That I walk with a sweet and girlish gait,
With my hips kind of swively and swervy.
I adore being dressed in something frilly
When my date comes to get me at my place.
Out I go with my Joe or John or Billy,
Like a filly who is ready for the race!

When I have a brand new hair-do,
With my eyelashes all in curl,
I float as the clouds on air do—
I enjoy being a girl!
When men say I'm cute and funny,
And my teeth aren't teeth, but pearl,
I just lap it up like honey—
I enjoy being a girl!
    I flip when a fellow sends me flowers,
    I drool over dresses made of lace,
    I talk on the telephone for hours
    With a pound and a half of cream upon my face!
I'm strictly a female female,
And my future, I hope, will be
In the home of a brave and free male
Who'll enjoy being a guy,
Having a girl like me!

When men say I'm sweet as candy
As around in a dance we whirl,
It goes to my head like brandy—
I enjoy being a girl.
When someone with eyes that smoulder,
Says he loves every silken curl

That falls on my ivory shoulder—
I enjoy being a girl!
    When I hear the complimentary whistle
    That greets my bikini by the sea,
    I turn and I glower and I bristle—
    But I'm happy to know the whistle's meant for me!
I'm strictly a female female,
And my future, I hope, will be
In the home of a brave and free male
Who'll enjoy being a guy,
Having a girl like me . . .

(*During applause she moves over to the bench and sits, singing thoughtfully*)
    There is some part of every girl in me,
    Though I try to be different from the others.
    We have all got a tendency to be,
    Very much like our sisters and our mothers.
    We have problems to solve at different ages—
    We grow older, and up they come again!
    They are always the same at different stages,
    And they have to do with how to handle men.

(*Lost in these contemplations,* LINDA *exits and, as she does, a group of dancers demonstrate her philosophy. First two girls of fourteen enter, primp and preen and admire themselves. A boy* WANG SAN *enters. They make a bee-line for him. He flees. They chase him off. A girl of eighteen enters. Two boys follow. [At this age, you see, it is the boys who chase the girls] They dance and show off for her. She shows only mild interest. Another boy dances on and dances off with her, leaving the first two chagrined. They are quickly consoled by the entrance of two girls, and soon the stage is filled with happy couples who dance gaily and romantically and quite briefly. As they exit,* WANG SAN *comes running on, still chased by the two lower teeners. As the three run off,* LINDA *returns and sings:)*

From men we may take an awful beating.
They're pains in our pretty little necks,
But all girls are interested in eating—
And we must have another sex to pay the checks!
I'm strictly a female female,
And my future, I hope, will be
In the home of a brave and free male
Who'll enjoy being a guy
Having a girl like me.

(TA *comes on with a sweater and holds it out stiffly.* LINDA *snuggles closely to* TA)

LINDA

Would you put it around me?
(TA *does*)
Now, where were we?

TA

We were talking about your ambition.

LINDA

Oh yes. What about yours?

TA

Well, it is difficult for a Chinese, even with a college degree, to find employment. I think I will study law, because then I won't have to look for a job for another three years.

LINDA

What will you do for money?

TA

My father.

LINDA

Is he rich?

TA

Very rich—and he really doesn't care what I do as long as I marry and give him grandchildren.

LINDA

He sounds very Chinese.

TA

Yes, he is completely Chinese, and that is good. It is good for my brother, he's completely American. But I am both, and sometimes the American half shocks the Oriental half, and sometimes the Oriental half keeps me from—showing a girl what is on my mind.

LINDA

Well, let's start working on the American half.
     (*Pause. Then* TA *takes the plunge*)

TA

Okay . . . Linda, will you marry me?

LINDA

Of course I'll marry you, but I'll have to ask my brother's consent.

TA

Let's go to him—now.

37

LINDA

He's on the ocean.

TA

When we get his consent, I will ask my father.

LINDA

Must we get his, too?

TA

Yes, that is my Chinese half—but I'm sure he will feel the same as I do about you.
    (THEY *kiss.* LINDA *resumes singing*)
        And my future, I hope, will be
        In the home of a brave and free male
        Who'll enjoy being a guy,
        Having a wife like me.
    (TA *puts his arm around* LINDA. *They walk upstage as the lights dim.*)

END OF SCENE TWO

ACT ONE

Scene 3

The WANG Living Room

AT RISE: WANG *stands on a footstool in the center of the stage. He wears a tweed coat minus one sleeve. The tailor,* LEE LUNG *is fitting the sleeve in place. Down Right,* MR. HUAN *of The Bank of America, Chinatown branch, sits with an iron chest in front of him, counting packages of neatly tied bills and putting them back in the chest.* SAN *sits behind him, watching, bug-eyed, at the stacks of money.* MADAM LIANG *looks on the fitting of* WANG'S *new "Western suit" with satisfaction.* WANG *is coughing, while* DR. LI *observes and listens with a worried expression.)*

DR. LI

That is a bad cough. I must get some herbs to cure it.

WANG

My cough gave me the authority I needed in this household. But what is my authority now? I am putting my money in a bank, and I am being measured for a foreign suit that itches my neck.

MADAM LIANG

Look at you in that Chinese Opera costume! You cannot even go to your son's Commencement.

TAILOR

(*Taking the coat off*)
I'll deliver the suit this evening. I know you'll wear it with great distinction.
(HE *has crossed on his last line to the door*)

WANG

Thank you Mr. Lung.
(*The* TAILOR *bows and exits*)

MR. HUAN

There are 87,700 dollars here by my calculation.

WANG

The man is honest.

MR. HUAN

Now, Mr. Wang Chi-Yang, since you wish to open an account with The Bank of America, will you give me your references?

WANG

(*Pointing to the money*)
There are my references—where are yours?

MR. HUAN

(*Starting for the door*)
Please drop by the bank any time.

WANG

Why? Must I go visit my money?
(*The* DOORBELL *rings.* DR. LI *who has risen and crossed up to open the door for* MR. HUAN, *now admits* HELEN CHAO. MR. HUAN *and* DR. LI *exit, leaving the door open.*)

MADAM LIANG

(*Bringing* HELEN *down*)

Helen Chao, I'm glad you came. Have you finished it?

HELEN CHAO

Yes—I worked late last night.

MADAM LIANG

You know Helen Chao, my seamstress. She made the gown for Ta to wear at his graduation.

WANG

(*Smiling*)

Ah yes, I am honored Miss Chao.

MADAM LIANG

You must give me the bill.

HELEN CHAO

Please, I have known Wang Ta since you first came to me— he was only a little fellow. I would like this to be a gift for his graduation.

MADAM LIANG

That is very good of you. Ta is waiting in his room.

HELEN

I will see if it fits.

(SHE *exits Left, followed by* MADAM LIANG)

WANG

She is very kind to your brother.

41

SAN

She's got a yen for him.

WANG

A yen?

SAN

That's when someone sends you—and Ta sends her.

WANG

What language are you speaking?

SAN

That's bop, pop!
(HE *exits, Right*)

DR. LI
(*Entering from the street*)
I put the bank man in a taxi.

WANG

Thank you, Dr. Li.
(*The* DOORBELL *rings and* DR. LI *admits* SAMMY FONG)

SAMMY

Good morning, Dr. Li—Master Wang. I just dropped in to
see how the kids are hitting it off.

WANG

My son was out last night. They have not met yet.

SAMMY

You'd better get them together if you want to meet that April
deadline.

42

MEI LI

(MEI LI *enters with the water pipe*)
I can come in? I have cleaned your water pipe.

WANG

Thank you, Mei Li.
(SHE *sees* SAMMY)

MEI LI

Hi, Sammy Fong.

SAMMY

Hi.
(WANG *starts to cough*)

MEI LI

Master Wang, you have another son somewhere? I have only
seen a little one.

WANG

(*Nods*)
He is in his room, dressing for his graduation.
(MASTER WANG *continues to cough*)

DR. LI

Mei Li—beat Master Wang's shoulders. It is good for the
cough.

WANG

Do you know how?

MEI LI

Oh yes, I used to beat my grandmother's when I was little.
(SHE *beats his shoulders, singing*)
   A hundred million miracles,

A hundred million miracles
Are happening every day.
I beat your neck behind the ear
And soon your cough will disappear
A hundred million. . . .
(TA *enters.* MEI LI *sees him and the song trails off. She slaps* WANG'S *shoulders weakly.*)

WANG

You are losing your strength, Mei Li. What happened?

SAMMY

(*Seeing her reaction to* TA)
A missile just hit the moon!

WANG

Oh—Dr. Li, this is my first-born, Wang Ta. (*Indicating* MEI LI) And this is his daughter, Mei Li.

TA

How do you do?

WANG

You know Mr. Fong?

SAMMY

Sure—how are you, Ta?

TA

Fine, thanks.

WANG

Dr. Li and his daughter are guests in our house.

TA

How long have you been in town, Mei Li?

MEI LI

Only for two days.

TA

Then you haven't seen anything much.

MEI LI

No, only a little of anything much.

TA

Do you like it here?

MEI LI

Oh yes, I like it—especially I like Quaker Oats!

WANG

My son, I am proud that you are the valedictorian of your class. What is your speech about? Read it to me.

(HELEN CHAO *enters and stands watching* TA *admiringly, as he reads his speech*)

TA

Today we are leaving the sheltering and protecting arms of our Alma Mater, and now we are entering a more turbulent life, where we will encounter new experiences, new associations. . . .

HELEN

Oh, that's wonderful, Wang Ta.

45

SAMMY

Wait till he warms up.

(MADAM LIANG *enters*)

MADAM LIANG

Excuse me. I am afraid we will be late for the Commencement.

(SHE *waves to* SAMMY FONG)

WANG

You may read it to us at the celebration tonight.

MEI LI

You are celebrating?

WANG

Two big events in our family.

MADAM LIANG

We are both graduating—I, from my Citizenship School.

HELEN

May I go to the graduation with you?

TA

Sure, come on.

(THEY *go off*)

WANG

Dr. Li, I am going to make a pilgrimage to the Temple of Tin How.

MEI LI

Will you be gone a long time?

46

WANG

No—it is just around the corner.

DR. LI

I, too, have reason to thank Tin How. Your son is a splendid young man. He does honor to your venerable name.

SAMMY

I'll give you a lift. I've got a car outside. I borrowed my girl's Thunderbird.

(WANG, DR. LI *and* SAMMY FONG *exit, leaving* MEI LI *alone onstage. She looks around the room well pleased with her surroundings*)
(SHE *sings:*)
I am going to like it here.
There is something about the place,
An encouraging atmosphere,
Like a smile on a friendly face.

There is something about the place,
So caressing and warm it is—
Like a smile on a friendly face,
Like a port in a storm it is!

So caressing and warm it is—
All the people are so sincere,
Like a port in a storm it is,
I am going to like it here!

All the people are so sincere,
There's especially one I like.
I am going to like it here.
It's the father's first son I like!

There's especially one I like,
There is something about his face.

FLOWER DRUM SONG

It's the father's first son I like
He's the reason I love the place.

There is something about his face,
I would follow him anywhere.
(SHE *sings more slowly*)
If he goes to another place . . .
I am going to like it there!
(SHE *picks up* TA'S *pipe, holds it affectionately against
her cheek, and sings again:*)
If he goes to another place. . . .
I am going to like it there!

END OF SCENE 3

ACT ONE

Scene 4

SCENE: WANG's *Bedroom*

The room is simply furnished with a few personal pieces that WANG *brought over from China. A single bed is placed against the wall, and to the right a four-foot teakwood screen used to shut off the room when* WANG *is napping. A few uncomfortable, straight-backed teakwood chairs, a small night table with a gold figure of a Chinese god, a water pipe, and several weighty volumes of Oriental lore complete the room.*

A portrait of the late MADAM WANG *hangs on the wall above the bed along with framed pictures of* WANG's *sons.*

AT RISE: *The door opens and* WANG *comes into the room, followed by* DR. LI. WANG *carries a large dress box under his arm, which he immediately starts to unpack.*

DR. LI

I told Mei Li to come up here as soon as she gets dressed.
(*Noticing portrait*)
That was the late Madam Wang?
(WANG *nods*)

49

WANG

She was a noble woman. My father arranged our marriage.
I will bless him for it all my life.

(WANG *has unpacked the box and holds up an evening
dress*)

DR. LI

What a surprise! I can't wait to see her expression. She has
never had anything like it before. Aiyoo! What will she say?

WANG

She will like it.

(*The* MEN *look at it, and notice the built-in pads for the
breasts*)

DR. LI

What are these things for?

WANG

All of the women over here have them.

DR. LI

At home our daughters are taught to strap themselves in—

WANG

Here, they let themselves out.

DR. LI

Maybe they serve to keep people away from them in crowds.

WANG

Whatever they're for, they all wear them in the United States.
Here it is a symbol, like the American Eagle.

(*There is a* KNOCK *at the door. The* MEN *exchange smiles and* WANG *conceals the dress behind his back*)

WANG

Come in.
(MEI LI *enters the room.* SHE *is dressed in a plain, light blue Chinese robe.*)

MEI LI

Good evening Master Wang—evening my father.
(WANG *nods and suppresses a smile*)
How do I look? Is this all right to wear at the party?
(THEY *look her over silently*)

DR. LI

You are not going to wear that dress.

MEI LI

(*Sadly*)
But Father, it is the best dress I have.

DR. LI

Our dear friend, Master Wang, has bought you a gift.
(WANG *holds the dress up in front of him*)

MEI LI

Oh! It is beautiful! Master Wang—how can I thank you?
(*Hugging the dress to her bosom as he hands it to her*)

WANG

Put it on, see if it fits.

DR. LI

The woman in the store was your size—

51

(MEI LI *goes behind the screen upstage*)
Your gift has made my child happy. It was very generous of
you.

WANG

No, it was not generous. It was my vanity. I wanted to do
honor to my guest.
(MADAM LIANG *barges in carrying the jacket of* MASTER
WANG's *Western suit. There is a large hole burned in the
lapel.*)

MADAM LIANG

What happened to your Western suit?

WANG

(*Suppressing a smile*)
I accidentally burned a hole in it while smoking my water pipe.

MADAM LIANG

Accidentally!
(*Holds up the coat, revealing a large hole*)
You let it burn long enough to cook a suckling pig!

WANG

Throw it away.

MADAM LIANG

You cannot throw away an expensive suit like this. I will send
it to Helen Chao the first thing in the morning. She will mend
it for you.
(MEI LI, *dressed in her new gown, steps from behind the
screen*)

52

MEI LI

Do I look like an American tomato?

WANG

What is that?

MEI LI

Wang San says Ta likes American tomatoes.
(TA *comes into the room. He is dressed in his dinner coat, and carries a small plastic box containing a corsage*)

TA

Father, I wanted to talk to you.

WANG

Come in, my son.
(TA *reacts as he sees* MEI LI)

MEI LI

Wang Ta, why do you stare at me?

TA

I didn't know you.

WANG

My son, what did you want to talk to me about?

TA

It is about a young friend and her brother I have asked to the party.

WANG

If they are friends of yours, they are welcome.

53

MADAM LIANG

I see you have brought flowers for Mei Li.

TA

(*Taken off balance—trapped*)

Oh—yes, of course.

(TA *presents the box of flowers to* MEI LI. *He has no choice*)

MEI LI

Thank you, Wang Ta.

MADAM LIANG

(*Turning to* DR. LI, *smiling*)

Over here it is the custom to "say it with flowers."

DR. LI

Say what with flowers?

MADAM LIANG

Anything they have on their minds.

LIU MA

(*Entering*)

The guests are beginning to arrive.

MADAM LIANG

(*To* WANG)

Come—help me greet them.

(SHE *takes* DR. LI's *arm and goes out with the two men, leaving* MEI LI *and* TA *alone.*)

(MEI LI *reaches up on tip-toe and pins a flower in* TA's *lapel*)

54

MEI LI

I think I say it with flowers, too.

TA

Thank you, Mei Li.

MEI LI

You are so tall. You have been growing a long time. How old are you, Wang Ta?

TA

Twenty-one.

MEI LI

In China, your father would have found you a wife three years ago.

TA

Here you are not really a man till you're twenty-one. Then you can choose your own wife.

MEI LI

Without your father?

TA

Yes.

MEI LI

How would you know if she is the right one for you?

TA

If she is the right one—when you are away from her you can't keep your mind off her. And when you are with her you can't

55

keep your hands off her. You cannot understand unless it happens to you.

MEI LI

But I *do* understand. It *has* happened to me.

TA

Who is the lucky man?

MEI LI

I will not tell him until he asks my father.
(*There is an embarrassing pause.* SHE *tries to relieve it*)
Wang San told me American joke. Would you like to hear?

TA

Yes. Go ahead.

MEI LI
(*Handing the plastic flower box to* TA)
Well—the first Space Ship landed on the moon and found people there. The people on the moon are so small, like a bean, they all fit in your hand. And a Space Man fell in love with a girl and asked her to marry.
(MEI LI *extends her hands indicating a hand for each.*
Addressing Right hand)
I love you. I want to marry you. I want to take you back to the earth. Ask your father?
(*Addressing Left hand*)
Sir, I would like to. . . .
(*To Right hand*)
Shhhhhhh—
(*To Left hand*)
I would like to marry with your daughter. Yes? May I?

(*Clasping hands together*)
Oh, that's wonderful!
(*Obviously the father and daughter have been squashed
by the happy lover. This is the joke and* TA *laughs. She
is delighted*)

MEI LI

How would you ask a girl to marry you, Ta? What would you
say?

TA

I'd say . . . . Darling—

MEI LI

That's nice.

TA

I'd say. Darling—

MEI LI

Yes?
(HE *sings:*)
   Am I the man that you love?
   If that is true, I am more,
   Something beyond and above,
   The man that I was before.

   Like a god
   With my head above the trees,
   I can walk with a god-like stride.
   With a step I can clear the seven seas,
   When I know you are by my side.
   Like a god
   With a mountain in my hand

57

And my arm thrown around the sky,
All the world
Can be mine at my command,
When you're near and I hear you sigh.
When you're near and I hear you sigh,
There is no sweeter song I know.
With a heart full of hope I fly,
Higher I go,
Stronger I grow!
Like a god I can tear away the mist
From the sky when you want it blue.
In the wake of the mist
Like a goddess you'll be kissed
By a god in love with you

(TA *looks down at her, then starts a second refrain*)

Like a god
With my head above the trees,
I can walk with a god-like stride.

(HE *exits but continues singing offstage.* MEI LI, *alone, imitates him and synchronizes her lips to his singing*)

With a step I can clear the seven seas,
When I know you are by my side.
Like a god
With a mountain in my hand
And my arm thrown around the sky.
All the world
Can be mine at my command,
When you're near and I hear you sigh.

(MEI LI *continues to gesture broadly for a moment before she realizes that* TA *has stopped singing.* SHE *gazes at the door—* SHE *is happy, walking on air.* SHE *begins to sing softly to herself*)

A hundred million miracles,

A hundred million miracles
Are happening every day.
And those who say they don't agree
Are those who cannot hear or see,
A hundred million miracles,
A hundred million miracles
Are happening every day.
(*While singing,* MEI LI *has been walking slowly to Right,
beating the plastic corsage box as she had beaten the
flower drum. As she exits the lights dim.*)

END OF SCENE 4

ACT ONE

Scene 5

SCENE: *The Garden of the* WANG *house. Night. Beyond the* WANG *house up center you can see the pagodas of Chinatown. The garden is lighted with Chinese lanterns.*

AT RISE: *There is applause heard behind the curtain, continuing as the curtain rises. Seated around the garden are the pupils of the Marina American Citizenship School, and* TA'S *friends. Seated up center are* WANG, MADAM LIANG *and* DR. LI. *As curtain rises* PROFESSOR CHENG *stands at the center of the stage holding up a medal. A boy is crossing to him.*

PROF. CHENG

Sam Kee Sing, it is my pleasure to present to you the Medal of Excellence for leading the Junior Division of the Marina School of American Citizenship.

(*Applause while* PROF. CHENG *pins medal on little boy, who kowtows, salutes and returns to his place.*)

Before making my final award, I wish to thank Master Wang Chi-Yang for so graciously permitting us to use his beautiful garden for our commencement exercises.

(*Applause—*WANG *bows*)

And now, I proudly announce the winner of the Senior Medal of Excellence. Madam Liang.

(*Applause while* MADAM LIANG *rises*)

PROF. CHENG

(*Pinning a medal on* MADAM LIANG)

Master Wang, aren't you proud to have such a fine American citizen in your family?

WANG

To become an American citizen it took her five years. She was Chinese in nine months.

MADAM LIANG

I am proud to be both Chinese and American.

WANG

You are like that Chinese dish that the Americans invented —what do they call it?

MADAM LIANG

Chop Suey?

WANG

That's it. Everything is in it, all mixed up.

MADAM LIANG

That is what is good about my new country. "Everything is in it—all mixed up," I like that!

    (SHE *sings:*)
        Chop Suey,
        Chop Suey,
        Living here is very much like Chop Suey:
        Hula Hoops and nuclear war,
        Doctor Salk and Zsa Zsa Gabor,
        Harry Truman, Truman Capote and Dewey—
        Chop Suey!

61

FLOWER DRUM SONG

Chop Suey!

MADAM LIANG

Stars are drifting overhead,
Birds and worms have gone to bed.

Men work late in laboratories,
Others read detective stories,

Some are roaming 'round the country,
Others sit beneath just *one* tree—

To-night on TV's late, late show,
You can look at Clara Bow!

ALL

Who? . . .
Chop Suey!
Chop Suey!
Good and bad, intelligent, mad and screwy,

MADAM LIANG

Violins and trumpets and drums—
Take it all the way that it comes.
Sad and funny, sour and honeydewy—

ALL

Chop Suey!

MADAM LIANG

Ball-Point pens and filter tips,
Lipsticks and potato chips!

62

GIRLS' QUARTET

In the dampest kind of heat wave
You can give your hair a neat wave.

MADAM LIANG

Hear that lovely La Paloma
Lullaby by Perry Coma!

SAN

Dreaming in my Maiden-Form Bra,
Dreamed I danced The Cha Cha Cha—

GIRLS	SAN *and* BOYS
Chop Suey,	Cha cha cha cha
Chop Suey,	Cha cha cha cha

ALL

Mixed with all the hokum and bally-hooey,

MADAM LIANG

Something real and glowing and grand
Sheds a light all over the land—

ALL

Boston, Austin, Wichita and St. Louis—
Chop Suey!
        Chop Suey!
Chop Suey!
        Chop Suey!
CHOP SUEY!

ALL

Weather chilly all through Philly,
Hot and clammy in Miami,

63

MADAM LIANG

Mississippi River swollen—
Mrs. Astor's fur is stolen,

ALL

No!

MADAM LIANG

Thinks a juvenile delinquent
Knows exactly where her mink went!

Doctor Norman Vincent Peale
Tells you how to feel—

ALL

Big deal!

Chop Suey,
Chop Suey,
Rough and tough and brittle and soft and gooey—

Peking Duck and Mulligan stew,
Plymouth Rock and Little Rock, too.

Milk and beer and Seven-Up and Drambuie—
Chop Suey
         Chop Suey
Chop Suey
         Chop Suey
CHOP SUEY!
(TA *and* MEI LI *enter, crossing to* MADAM LIANG *and
group of girls who are admiring her medal*)

TA

You're wonderful, Aunt Liang.

MEI LI

I congratulate you, Madam Liang, for your noble decoration.
(SHE *fingers medal*)

MADAM LIANG

Thank you, my dear.

MEI LI

I would like to go to school too. . . .
(LINDA LOW *and her "brother"* FRANKIE *enter.* LINDA *is
stunningly dressed and* FRANKIE *is a handsome naval officer in full regalia.* TA *sees them, over* MEI LI's *head,
and it is apparent that he is not listening to* MEI LI *as
she continues to talk*)
. . . and when I get decorated. . . . you will be proud of me.

TA

Excuse me, Mei Li.
(HE *makes a beeline for* LINDA)

LINDA

Hi, Ta! My brother, Commodore Low.
(TA *acknowledges the introduction and leads them down
to his family*)

TA

May I present my father, Madam Liang, Dr. Li and his
daughter, Mei Li—Miss Linda Low and her brother Commodore Low.

LINDA

Hi, everybody!

SAN

You're the Thunderbird!

65

LINDA

That's me.

MEI LI

(*Sniffing*)
Sweet incense! you smell good.

LINDA

My brother brings it to me from Paris.

MEI LI

You use incense to keep evil spirits away?

LINDA

No—to attract them!
(TA *tries to smile, and looks at his father who is not amused*)

WANG

You live with your family, Miss Low?

LINDA

No, I have a little apartment on Grant Avenue—near my music teacher.

WANG

You are a student?

SAN

You sing Rock and Roll?

LINDA

I like anything cukey. I dig that the most.

66

SAN

Do you know "You be the rock, I'll be the roll? . . ."

LINDA

Sure!
> (*Singing and dancing with* WANG SAN)
>> You be the rock
>> I'll be the roll,
>> You be the soup,
>> I'll be the bowl.
>> You be the furnace,
>> I'll be the coal—rock, rock, rock!

WANG

> (*Impatiently*)

Wang San!
> (SAN *stops abruptly*)

SAN

> (*Nudging* LINDA)

Strictly—
> (SAN *draws a square with his hands for* LINDA's *benefit and exits upstage*)
> (LIU MA *enters and hits the dinner gong three times*)

MADAM LIANG

Please, everyone, there are things to eat in the dining hall.
> (*The guests start off. Left on the stage are* TA, LINDA, DR. LI, FRANKIE, MEI LI *and* WANG. WANG *starts to go.* LINDA *prods* FRANKIE, *indicating* WANG)

FRANKIE

Master Wang—Venerable Master Wang,
> (*Memorizing what he has been told to say*)

67

I wish to say that I have been considering your son's proposal to my honorable sister.

(*A shocked reaction from* WANG, MEI LI, DR. LI *and* MADAM LIANG)

WANG

Proposal!
(HE *looks at* TA *quickly*)

FRANKIE

As her guardian and her loving brother, I hereby give my consent.

LINDA

(*Rushing over to* WANG)
Father!
(SHE *plants a good smack of lipstick on his cheek*)

FRANKIE

(*To* WANG)
Do you give *your* consent?
(WANG *has been knocked off his feet and is confused and unable to cope with this sudden development. In cases like this he always coughs. When he starts to cough,* MEI LI *runs over to* WANG *and starts to beat his shoulders the way she did before.* WANG *interrupts.*)

WANG

Please—I would like to speak to my son alone.
(*There is an appeal in his voice which is not missed by* LINDA, *who nods to her "brother."* THEY *exit. As they start off,* MEI LI *goes to her father*)

68

MEI LI

I am going to my room, my father. I think I want to go to bed.

DR. LI

I understand.

(DR. LI *puts his arm around* MEI LI *and goes off with her, passing* MADAM LIANG *who remains on, in the background. After a pause* WANG *addresses his son*)

WANG

This woman's brother speaks of a proposal.

TA

(*Speaking with great effort*)
I have asked Miss Low to marry me.

WANG

What do you know of marriage? What do you know of women?

TA

Sir, what did *you* know of marriage and of women when you married my mother?

WANG

Nothing! That is why I obeyed my father and married the woman he chose for me.

TA

Sir, I have to tell you that I love Miss Low and I want to marry her. After all, I am twenty-one.

WANG

Do you think you were born twenty-one? Almost all of what

you are up to now has come from me. I have given you my
daily concern, my teaching—

TA

Anytime I wanted to do anything, *you* decided it for me.

WANG

That is as it should be.

TA

In China—yes. But here a man is supposed to think for himself.

WANG

While you are in my house, you will live the life I have designed for you. When the day comes that you can think for
yourself, I will let you know!

(WANG *exits.* WANG SAN *and a girl come on from Left*)

MADAM LIANG

Wang San, go up to Mei Li's room and tell her your brother
would like to see her in the garden.

(WANG SAN *nods and he and the girl hurry into the
house.*)

(MADAM LIANG *crosses down to* WANG TA *who sits de-
jectedly on a bench*)

MADAM LIANG

My nephew, your father is a wise man and I—

TA

(*Interrupting*)

Oh, he's wise all right! Every time he doesn't want to give
you an answer, he has a coughing spell.

70

MADAM LIANG

I know. Sometimes he drives me crazy too, but I let him have his cough. It is the only weapon he has to fight back with over here.

TA

That is why he will never let a doctor cure it.

MADAM LIANG

I think you have hurt our little house guest, too.

TA

Mei Li? How?

MADAM LIANG

First you bring her flowers—

TA

That was your idea. I brought them for Linda Low.

MADAM LIANG

Mei Li has gone to her room. I have sent Wang San for her. While she is in our house, you must be nice to her.
(MADAM LIANG *sees* MEI LI *coming from the house. She pats* TA's *shoulder and goes off.*)
(MEI LI *is now dressed in a silk pajama coat and pants.* SHE *comes down to* TA *gingerly*)

MEI LI

Wang San said you wanted to see me.

TA

I didn't know where you were.

71

MEI LI

I went to my room. I didn't want to see you unhappy with
your father . . . He did not give consent? Is there something
I can do for you?

TA

No, Mei Li. Thanks anyway.
(SAMMY FONG *enters from the house smiling happily*)

SAMMY FONG

How are the love birds? Don't tell me, I can see. Everybody's
eating and you're not—a good sign.

TA

How are you Sammy? Will you excuse me? I think I'd better
look after my guests.
(HE *exits*)

SAMMY

You're getting a fine fellow—handsome, intelligent, good family—and loaded.

MEI LI

I have not got him. He is in love with another girl.

SAMMY

What? Don't tell me he'd pass you up for one of these local
egg-rolls?

MEI LI

She is a very pretty egg-roll.

SAMMY

So what? You're quite an appetizer yourself! Now listen, baby,
if she takes Ta away from you, his father will throw that con-

tract right back in my lap. You'd better get on the ball, baby,
or you're going to be stuck with me!

(SAMMY *sings*)

>You are young and beautiful,
>Sweet as the breath of May.
>Earnestly I speak to you—
>Weigh every word I say:
>
>If you want to have a rosy future
>And be happy as a honey bee
>With a husband who will always love you, baby,
>Don't marry me!
>If you want a man you can depend on,
>I can absolutely guarantee
>I will never fail to disappoint you, baby,
>Don't marry me!
>>I eat litchi nuts and cookies in bed,
>>And I fill the bed with nutshells and crumbs.
>>I have irritating habits you'll dread,
>>Like the way I have of cracking my thumbs!
>My grandpa was a big game hunter,
>He met grandma swinging on a tree—
>If you want to have attractive children, baby,
>Don't marry me!

(*They dance*)

MEI LI

>I would like to see my sons and daughters
>Sliding up and down their father's knee—

SAMMY

>They'll get splinters in their little fannies, cookie,
>Don't marry me.
>I'm devoted to my dear old mama

And if you and mama disagree,
I would always side with her against you, schnookie,
Don't marry me.

MEI LI
I would always like to know where you go.
I don't like a man to keep me in doubt—

SAMMY
Honey, that's a thing that's easy to know—
You will always know where *I* am, I'm out!
I am talking like a Chinese uncle,
I'm as serious as I can be,
I am saying this because I love you, darling,
Don't marry me!
Marry a dope,
Innocent and gaga.
Marry a Khan—
Ali or the Aga.
Marry for money
Or marry for free,
BUT DON'T MARRY ME!

MEI LI
(*Speaking, after a pause.*)
I accept your proposal not to marry me, but you must ask my
father.
(MEI LI *exits while* SAMMY *tries to figure it out*)
(LINDA LOW *comes on with* WANG SAN, *followed by* COM-
MODORE LOW, *with a girl on each arm.* SAMMY FONG *re-
acts as he sees them*)

SAN
Hello, Mr. Fong.

SAMMY

Hello, Wang San. Who's your friend?

(COMMODORE LOW *and* LINDA *exchange glances*)

SAN

Miss Linda Low—and her brother, Commodore Low—this is Mr. Sammy Fong.

(SAMMY *walks slowly over to* "COMMODORE LOW," *who would like to drop through the floor*)

SAMMY

Who's taking tickets down at the theatre? Hi, Commodore, glad to have you aboard.

COMMODORE

Thanks.

SAMMY

What's the name of your ship?

COMMODORE

The S.S. . . . . S.S.—
(HE *hesitates*)

SAMMY

Well, you got the initials right anyway. Let me wish you bon voyage before you shove off!

COMMODORE

Thanks.
(HE *hurries off Left*)

LINDA

Did you say the name was Fong?

75

SAMMY

Yeah.

LINDA

(*As if trying to remember where she has heard the name*)
Fong, Fong, Fong. . . .

SAMMY

Those are my uncles.
(WANG SAN *goes off with the two girls* COMMODORE LOW
escorted, leaving SAMMY FONG *and* LINDA *alone*)

SAMMY

What are you doing here?

LINDA

I've got news for you, Sammy. . . . Ta and I are engaged to
be married.

SAMMY

Are you on a security kick? Getting yourself engaged to a kid
just because he was born with silver chop-sticks in his mouth!

LINDA

You're jealous because you were only born with teeth!

SAMMY

Haven't you any feeling for the five years I've wasted on you?

LINDA

Sure—but I don't want to share you with a picture bride.
(GIRLS *and* BOYS *drift on*)

76

ACT ONE SCENE 5

GIRL

Linda! We heard you are going to marry Wang Ta.

LINDA

That's the general idea.

SAMMY

Yeah, she's on her way up. She'll wind up in a mansion on Nob Hill.
(*To* LINDA)
I know you have the good wishes of all Chinatown . . . and you know what I wish you.

LINDA

(*Sarcastically*)
Thanks, Mr. Fang!
(SAMMY *goes off*)

GIRL

Are you going to move to Nob Hill?

LINDA

No, I'm not moving from where I am—marriage or no marriage. I've got to be where the action is.

GIRL

Where is that?

LINDA

(*Singing:*)
Grant Avenue, San Francisco, California, U.S.A.—
Looks down
From Chinatown
Over a foggy bay.

77

You travel there in a trolley, in a trolley up you climb—
Dong Dong!
You're in Hong Kong,
Having yourself a time.
> You can eat, if you are in the mood,
> Shark-fin soup, bean cake fish.
> The girl who serves you all your food
> Is another tasty dish!
You know you
Can't have a new way of living till you're living all the
way
On Grant Avenue

ALL

Where is that?

LINDA

San Francisco,
That's where's that!
California,
U.S.A.

A Western street with Eastern manners
Tall pagodas and golden banners
Throw their shadows through the lantern glow.
You can shop for precious jade or
Teakwood tables or silk brocade or
See a bold and brassy night club show,
On the most exciting thoroughfare I know.
They call it—
(LINDA *sings another* REFRAIN, *followed by an* ENSEMBLE
DANCE)

END OF SCENE 5

ACT ONE

Scene 6

LINDA's *dressing room at the Celestial Bar.*

SCENE: *There is a dressing table and mirror, Left. Across the back wall, over a bench, hang her various costumes. A door, Right, leads outside.*

AT RISE: HELEN CHAO *is making a last minute repair on one of* LINDA's *costumes.* SAMMY FONG *comes into the room and looks around angrily.*

SAMMY

Where is she? Didn't she get back yet?

HELEN

She went to a party at the Wangs to meet her future in-laws.

SAMMY

Oh—so *you* were in on it too! Everybody knew it but me! Gee, you'd think I was a regular husband.

HELEN

Do you know the man she is marrying?

SAMMY

Man? He's a kid! I'll break his rice bowl.

HELEN

What are you going to do?

SAMMY

Stick around. You'll see.
> (*There is a knock at the door*)

Come in.
> (*A headwaiter enters*)

WAITER

Frankie said you were looking for me, Mr. Fong.

SAMMY

Yes. Keep that floor table for a party of five—for the first show
. . . and no check. It's on the house.

WAITER

What name, Mr. Fong?

SAMMY

Master Wang Chi-Yang and his family. I'll be out there.
> (WAITER *nods and goes*)

HELEN

Oh. I see.

SAMMY

You can *see*, but you didn't *hear* anything. Do you understand?
> (HELEN *nods*)
> (LINDA *comes in and stops abruptly as she sees* SAMMY
> FONG.)

LINDA

What are *you* doing in my dressing room?

SAMMY

Miss Chao, will you please step outside for a moment?

HELEN

Yes, Mr. Fong.
   (SHE *exits*)

SAMMY

   (*Putting on an act*)
I was a bum sport tonight. I've been thinking it over and I want to wish you luck.

LINDA

   (*Softens*)
Do you mean it, Sammy?

SAMMY

   (*Slyly*)
Sure I mean it! Outside of me, you're getting the finest kid in San Francisco.

LINDA

He's a little young.

SAMMY

He'll age!

LINDA

   (*Reminiscently*)
We've had some good times together.

SAMMY

   (*Nostalgically*)
Yeah, for five years. Boy, what memories!

LINDA

Sammy, would you mind if I quit tonight?

SAMMY

(*Worried*)
Tonight? Why?

LINDA

On account of Ta.

SAMMY

(*Recovering his outward calm*)
Sure, kid. But just do the first show.

LINDA

Please, Sammy—

SAMMY

(*Sentimentally*)
I want to see you work for the last time. I'll make a deal with
you. Go on for the first show and I'll keep up the payments
on the car.

LINDA

It's a deal.
(SHE *holds out her hand.* SAMMY *takes it and kisses her*)

SAMMY

That's my girl. I'll be watching you. I want to be out there
for your entrance.
(SAMMY *takes boutonniere and with an exaggerated, ro-
mantic air tosses it to* LINDA.)
I wish it were diamonds.

LINDA

So do I.
(SAMMY *exits.* HELEN *re-enters*)

HELEN

(*As she helps* LINDA *take off her dress*)
Has Wang Ta ever seen your act here?

LINDA

No, he doesn't even know I work here. That's the reason I'm quitting tonight.

HELEN

I have known him for ten years. I have watched him grow up into a fine, sensitive young man. He is not like the white Chinese born here. At heart he is an Oriental.

LINDA

(*As she puts on a dressing gown*)
You sound like you wish you could hook him yourself.

HELEN

(*With a sad laugh*)
Do I?
(LINDA *exits.* HELEN *sings:*)
        I have wished before
        I will wish no more . . .

    Love, look away!
    Love, look away from me.
    Fly, when you pass my door,
    Fly and get lost at sea.
    Call it a day.
    Love, let us say we're through,

83

FLOWER DRUM SONG

No good are you for me,
No good am I for you.
>Wanting you so, I try too much.
>After you go, I cry too much.
Love, look away.
Lonely though I may be,
Leave me and set me free,
Look away, look away, look away from me.

END OF SCENE 6

ACT ONE

Scene 7

The Celestial Bar

SCENE: *It is a typical San Francisco Chinese night club designed to attract tourists.*

    Up center is an alcove for a small band unit, flanked by narrow arches through which the performers in the show make their entrances and exits. There is a bar Right Center, and extending from the walls Right and Left are booths with pagoda roof lines. A large table down Left is where the WANG *family and guests will sit, later.*

AT RISE: *A chorus of girls in idealized coolie costumes are dancing to the accompaniment of a girl singer who blasts out the following Chinatown song:*

> Fan Tan Fanny
> Was leaving her man,
> Fan Tan Fanny
> Kept waving her fan,
> Said "Good-bye, Danny
> You two-timing Dan,
> Some other man
> Loves your little Fanny!
>   Bye, Bye!
> In the ice-box
> You'll find in a can,

85

Some left-overs
Of Moo-Goo-Guy-Pan.
Fan Tan Fanny
Has found a new guy,
His name is Manny,
He's good for Fanny,
So good-bye Danny,
Good-bye."

(*As the dancing girls are making their exit,* WANG CHI-YANG, DR. LI, MEI LI, MADAM LIANG *and* WANG TA *enter.*)

SAMMY FONG

(*Ushering them to a table, Left*)

Welcome to the Celestial Bar. I know you're going to enjoy the show.

(*To* WAITER)

Bring a magnum of Bollinger to this table.

(*As they are being seated* FRANKIE WING, *now in a dinner coat, comes on to a loud fanfare.* HE *picks up a mobile microphone and walks downstage.*)

FRANKIE

Hi folks! Welcome to the Celestial Bar. It does this old heart good to see so many smiling and distinguished faces. You look like a great audience to work to, and you're going to see a show tonight that will make the old hills of San Francisco rock with gaiety. A funny thing happened on the way here tonight—

(HE *breaks off suddenly as* HE *sees the family party of* WANG. *He is completely thrown by this sudden development*)

. . . I can't think what it was, but it struck me funny at the time.

MEI LI

(*Naively*)

It's Commodore Low!

(SHE *waves to him*)

(*The* WAITER *has started to pour champagne into glasses.* WANG *glares at his son.* FRANKIE *signals the orchestra and barges right into the opening song of the show*)

FRANKIE

I am a vagabond sailor . . .

All my friends call me sport—

(*He giggles nervously and looks encouragingly at* WANG, *trying to win a responsive smile.* WANG'S *face is stern and frozen.* FRANKIE *crosses the night club floor to what he hopes may be a more vulnerable audience. He stops in front of a boy and girl, sitting in a booth*)

I am a fellow for action,

Any storm in a port—

(*Speaking, laughing at the joke*)

Any storm in a port—get it?

(*The boy and girl are stony-faced.* FRANKIE *moves quickly away, muttering:*)

Back to the laundry.

(*At stage Center, he resumes singing:*)

Now that I'm home and I'm resting,

Home from over the sea,

All of the girls who adored me

Go gliding through my memoree!

(*The girls he refers to in the following refrain, enter one by one, on cue, from the upper arches. In spite of his descriptions of them they are all undeniably Asian*)

A sweet colleen from Ireland,

Her hair was fiery red,

87

Her eyes gave out a green light
That said I could go ahead.
(*Holding a microphone before her mouth*)
Say something Irish.

"IRISH" GIRL

Ellin go blah.

FRANKIE

I met a girl in Sweden
Of whom I grew quite fond,
A stately Scandinavian type,
A buxom, blue-eyed blonde—
(*As this very dark, unstately and unbuxom girl enters,
the "Irish" girl, standing only a few inches from* WANG
*treats him to a swing of her hip that jerks him up into
a sitting posture that is even more rigid than it was.*)
And then, in merry England,
A girl who worshipped me,
Gliding through my memoree—
That's how I see them,
Gliding through my memoree!
(*The three girls glide past him, and the next series enter,
as he describes them*)
In sunny Barcelona,
A dancing chick I picked.
Her castanets were clicking
Like nothing ever clicked!

GIRL

Olé!

FRANKIE

(*Speaking*)
You can say that again!

88

(*Singing*)
  'Twas fun to cast an anchor
  In lovely Casablanker.
  I loved a Grecian doll and
  Another doll in Holland,
  But of all the girls in every hemisphere,
  There is no one like the girl I have right here—
(LINDA *enters, oozing gaiety and confidence*)
  Right here on . . .

LINDA

(*Singing:*)
  Grant Avenue, San Francisco, California, U.S.A.—
(*As she continues with the song,* FRANKIE *makes frantic gestures and signals to her, trying to warn her of the presence of* WANG TA *and his family. She waves him off, as if she thinks he's kidding her and she's not going to be taken in.*)
(*The occupants of the* WANG *table have spotted her.* WANG *and* MADAM LIANG *glare at* TA, *whose head is lowered in deep humiliation. Things get worse when the number develops into a strip tease,* LINDA *and the chorus shedding their clothing in the traditional manner as the song progresses.*)
(LINDA *crosses to the Left not looking where she's going, and on the line, another tasty dish rips off her bodice, a foot or two in front of* WANG'S *face! Then she realizes what* FRANKIE'S *signals have meant! Too late!* WANG *has had enough. He rises and walks out, straight across the floor, through the chorus of stripping dancers.* MADAM LIANG *quickly follows. So do* DR. LI *and* MEI LI. TA *is left alone, disconsolate and stunned.* SAMMY *sitting at the*

*other end of the table has been a cool and satisfied ob-
server of all this, his handiwork.)*

*(LINDA continues with the number because she has to,
belting out the lyric even louder than before. Now, it is
HELEN CHAO'S moment and she recognizes it. She comes
down to TA, puts a sympathetic hand on his shoulder, puts
her other hand in his and leads him away. He follows
her, glad to have any help he can get in escaping from
the scene, glad to have some place else to go, with someone—anyone. HELEN throws back a quiet smile of triumph
towards LINDA, as she leads TA off.)*

*(SAMMY FONG takes a ringside seat at the WANG table
and catching LINDA'S eye as she sings, lifts his champagne glass in a mock toast. This is more than she can
stand. She picks up an ice bucket, pours it over SAMMY'S
head, places the whole bucket over his head and stalks
out, song or no song, public or no public. The girls go
on with the number more exuberantly than ever. SAMMY
slowly takes the bucket off his head. His hair, his face
and his evening coat are very wet indeed, probably cold,
too.)*

CURTAIN OF ACT ONE

Flower Drum Song

Act II

ACT TWO

Scene 1

HELEN CHAO'S *Room*

SCENE: *A modestly furnished room with an open kitchenette, up Right Center; a door to the hall, Left Center. On the Left wall is a bed, on the Right wall a door to the bathroom. Below this is a sewing machine, a telephone on the wall above it. In the center of the room, a table with a bottle of wine on it, a chair on either side.*

AT RISE: TA, *in his shirtsleeves, is pacing up and down the room angrily and a little unsteadily. He has a glass of wine in his hand. After taking a drink he turns to* HELEN.

TA

What do you call this stuff, Helen?

HELEN

Tiger Bone wine.

TA

Tiger Bone wine? I may make this a steady diet from now on.
(HE *resumes his angry pacing*)
What a damn fool I made of myself. . . . Her brother gave her the Thunderbird—to save carfare!

93

HELEN

She has no brother. Sammy Fong gave her that. He gave her everything she's got. She's been his girl for five years.

TA

Sammy Fong's girl!

(HE *paces again*)

The worst part of it is, it proves my father was right. How am I going to face him? Maybe I won't have to. I'll call him.

(As HE *dials phone*)

Helen, give me another drink please?

(SHE *pours a good drink and* HE *gulps it down, as* HE *answers phone*)

Oh—hello my aunt . . . is Father awake? Oh, he isn't? . . . No—no don't wake him, it may put him in a bad humor . . . He did?

(*Cups phone. To* HELEN)

He coughed all the way home from the night club!

(*Into phone*)

I'm all right. I'm at someone's house . . . no, I'm with a fraternity brother . . . I'll be home in a little while.

(HE *hangs up, crosses to the chair, Left, to get his dinner jacket*)

Thanks, Helen, I don't know what I would have done without you.

HELEN

(As he weaves unsteadily)

Ta, you can't go out like that. Lie down. Rest awhile. I will call a taxi for you and wake you when it comes.

(*She leads him to the bed. He slumps down on the bed, taking off his tie and loosening his collar. He is practically "out." His eyes blink, droop and close.* HELEN *tiptoes away with his jacket.*)

TA

(*Singing sleepily and a little off key:*)

She is beautiful, small and shy.

(*His eyes close. The lights dim off, leaving him in a spot-light. As one in a trance, he rises and walks downstage, murmuring:*)

She is beautiful. . . .

(*The set breaks up and slides offstage. Lights come up slowly, revealing a drop on which is painted an impression of a Chinese landscape.* TA's *nightmare is now depicted by a ballet in which he becomes involved first with a dancer who symbolizes* MEI LI, *then with another who represents* LINDA. *In each case he is frustrated by entrances of other dancers who come between him and his desires. He ends up crouched in fear and confusion before "*LINDA,*" "*MEI LI*" and many others milling around him and whirling menacingly in front of him. Suddenly they disappear and leave the lone figure of* HELEN CHAO *who comes down towards him, dressed in an enticing negligee. She slips into his arms. He picks her up, kisses her and carries her off. The lights dim to a blackout.*)

(*The set is restored in the dark. When the lights come up, it is morning.* HELEN *is laying out a breakfast. There is a knock on the door. She answers it, admitting* MEI LI.)

MEI LI

Good morning, Miss Helen Chao.

HELEN

(*Nervously*)

Good morning, Miss Mei Li.

MEI LI

(*Holding up* WANG's *coat*)
Madam Liang asked me to bring the old Master's Western suit.
It is damaged.

> (HELEN *takes it and holds it up, revealing the hole* WANG
> *has burned in it. Meanwhile* MEI LI's *eyes light on* TA's
> *evening jacket hanging over the back of a chair. It still
> has the flower she gave him in its lapel.*)

HELEN

Excuse me a minute.

> (*She goes over to the bathroom door and closes it*)

How did he do that?

MEI LI

He said it burned easily.

> (HELEN *takes the coat and hangs it from a coathanger on
> the wall. As she does this,* MEI LI *glides into the room,
> takes the flower out of* TA's *jacket and hides it behind
> her. She addresses* HELEN *as she comes back to her*)

Please tell Madam Liang when it is ready, and I will come
and get it.

HELEN

Yes, I will Miss Mei Li. Thank you. Good-bye.

> (HELEN *edges* MEI LI *to the door, and* MEI LI *goes out.*)

HELEN

(*Opening the door*)
You can come out now.

> (TA *crosses to the bed, and picks up his shoes.*)

There was a customer here. I am preparing breakfast for you.

> (HE *sits and starts to put on his shoes*)

96

TA

Thanks, but I can't wait. It's past noon.

HELEN

It won't take a minute. It is not good to go out empty.

TA

No, thank you. I must go, Helen. My father has probably called the police, and every hospital in town. I've never stayed out all night before.

HELEN

Ta, if you will come to see me again, I will cook a dinner for you. I am a good cook, and no one ever tastes my cooking.

TA

Thanks, I'd like to sometime.

HELEN

When?

TA

Soon.

HELEN

If we could see each other once in a while, it would mean a great deal to me . . . it gets so lonely sometimes. . . . Look around you. This is the room I live in and work in.

TA

Why don't you go out more?

HELEN

You can't go out at night alone.

TA

You must have friends.

HELEN

Not *any* that I care about.
(*By this time,* TA *has tied his shoes.* HE *rises and* HELEN
ties his tie as she continues her speech)
I would love to go out with you sometime.

TA

Sure. We'll do that sometime.
(*Looking at his watch*)
Gosh, I have got to go. I'll call you Helen.
(*Putting on his jacket*)

HELEN

Do you know my number?

TA

I'll get it from my aunt.

HELEN

No. Don't ask her. Here is one of my cards.
(SHE *gives him a business card*)

TA

Thanks.
(HE *puts it down on the bed while he puts on his rain-
coat.*)
Good-bye, Helen.
(*He waves to her and leaves. She sees the card he left
behind, picks it up and runs to the door. Then she stops
in her tracks, realizing the pathetic futility of pressing*

98

*her attentions on a man who is so obviously not inter-
ested. She turns and walks downstage, letting the card
drop from her hand.)*

HELEN

(Singing:)
   . . . Call it a day,
   Love let us say we're through.
   No good are you for me,
   No good am I for you.
   Wanting you so, I try too much.
   After you go, I cry too much!
   Love look away,
   Lonely though I may be,
   Leave me and set me free.
   Look away, look away, look away from me.

END OF SCENE ONE

ACT TWO

Scene 2

SCENE: WANG's *Living Room*

Noon that day.

AT RISE: MADAM LIANG *is seated at the table sewing.* WANG *is pacing up and down agitatedly smoking his water pipe.*

WANG

I want you to ask the Police Department of the Executive Department to close down that night club!

MADAM LIANG

They cannot. It is a free enterprise.

WANG

It is destroying public morals. That she-demon throwing her evil spirits in our faces.

MADAM LIANG

That is an American Folk Dance.

WANG

It is bad luck to have a woman shake her naked body at you.
(*There is a noise at the door.*)

100

MADAM LIANG

It's Ta!

(WANG SAN *enters the room. He is wearing a baseball shirt and carries a baseball glove in his hand.*)

WANG

Why are you not in school?

SAN

It is Saturday.

WANG

Always some excuse!

MADAM LIANG

Go get your lunch.

SAN

Why don't we ever have sandwiches?

WANG

Raw meat on bread? Only cannibals eat raw meat, and if you want to be one, move to the hills and live like a cannibal!

(WANG SAN *shrugs and exits Right*)

Another citizen for your Western world! This is the first time Ta has ever stayed away all night. What could he be doing?

MADAM LIANG

If this was a quiz program I could win a trip to Europe.

WANG

When I lived at home with my parents, I never stayed away all night.

(HE *sings:*)

    I am puzzled by the attitude

Of children over here.
They are often disobedient
They seem to have no fear
    Of the father.

MADAM LIANG

They come home when they are tired out
Or when they want to eat.
And they act as if their coming home
Were quite a special treat
    For the father.

WANG

My older son, at twenty-one, has just discovered love,
A complicated subject he knows very little of.

MADAM LIANG

Your younger son confuses me, the way he uses words,
He tells me I am "cukey" and "something for the birds!"

WANG

What are we going to do about
The Other Generation?

MADAM LIANG

How will we ever communicate
Without communication?

WANG

You don't know where they go, or what they do—

MADAM LIANG

And what peculiar thoughts they think,
They never reveal to you.

WANG

A very discouraging problem is
The Other Generation
They want to lead a life that's all their own.

MADAM LIANG

Perhaps we ought to let them,
Forsake them and forget them!
But then we'd only find ourselves alone

TOGETHER

With one another!
I don't believe we'd like to be alone!

WANG

When you speak from your experience
You meet with cool disdain.
Every child is born with knowledge
Beyond the puny brain
      Of a father.

MADAM LIANG

Every child is born with confidence
A parent can't achieve
And the kind of intuition
That compels him to believe
      What he'd rather.

WANG

My older son has chosen a daughter-in-law for me,
A dancer in a night club is my daughter-in-law to be!

MADAM LIANG

She dances and undresses till she's naked as a flea—
And everyone can look at—

TOGETHER

What he alone should see!

What are we going to do about
The Other Generation?
How will we ever communicate
Without communication?

MADAM LIANG

They never take the blame for one mistake,

WANG

Oh no!
Their parents are responsible
For every mistake they make!

TOGETHER

A very discouraging problem is
The Other Generation
And soon there'll be another one as well!

MADAM LIANG

And when our out-of-hand sons
Are bringing up our grandsons,
I hope our grandsons give their fathers hell!

WANG

Can't wait to see it!

TOGETHER

I hope our grandsons give their fathers hell!

DR. LI

(Entering)
Is Mei Li back yet?

WANG

No. Not yet.
> (*There is a noise at the door*)

WANG and MADAM LIANG

It's Ta!
> (TA *lets himself into the room.* HE *nods sheepishly to his father and aunt.*)

MADAM LIANG

So—it is finally you!

WANG

Where have you been till this hour?
> (TA *starts to answer, but is silenced by* WANG)

Stop! Not in front of your aunt!

TA

I humbly beg your forgiveness for last night.

WANG

I have many things to say to you, but anything I say now, you have already said to yourself.

TA

I should have listened, my father.

WANG

Finding the right woman is a responsibility that rests on my shoulders—and I am happy to say I have found her.

TA

You've chosen a wife for me?

FLOWER DRUM SONG

MADAM LIANG

Your father has spoken to Dr. Li.

DR. LI

(*To* TA)
I would be honored to have you for my son-in-law.

WANG

(*Opening a decanter*)
We shall drink to the happiness of our children with Tiger
Bone wine.
(TA *reacts, remembering the previous night*)

DR. LI

(*As* MEI LI *enters through front door*)
Ah, my daughter, I am glad you are here.

MADAM LIANG

Mei Li, you must have some too.
(DR. LI *gives* MEI LI *a filled glass*)

WANG

To our grandchildren!
(WANG, MADAM LIANG *and* DR. LI *drink.* MEI LI *does not
drink, nor does* TA)

TA

Please, may I speak to Mei Li alone?

WANG

Yes, my son.
(WANG, DR. LI *and* MADAM LIANG *start off, Left*)

MADAM LIANG

Ta, did you know that Mei Li was born in the year of the rabbit?

WANG

And Ta was born in the year of the sheep. A perfect match—
(*The three older people exit.* TA *and* MEI LI *are left on-stage*)

TA

My father has chosen you to be my wife. I am honored to obey his wish.

MEI LI

Yesterday I was happy in the hope that he would choose me. I walked around the house wanting to sing songs to myself. Once or twice I *did* sing.
(SHE *looks away from him*)
Then I learned it was another girl you wanted.

TA

That's over. You were at the Celestial Bar last night. You saw what a fool I made of myself.

MEI LI

I am thinking not only of last night. This morning, I took your father's coat to Helen Chao's to be mended.
(SHE *pauses and looks at him.* TA *begins to guess what's coming*)
I saw another coat on a chair, and these flowers!
(SHE *brings the flowers from behind her back and gives them to him*)
You will not understand how I feel unless I tell you something. It will be hard to say. . . .
(SHE *has difficulty in actually making the confession*)

When I first saw you, when you came into this room dressed in your graduation robe—

(HER *voice seems to fail her*)

TA

(*Encouraging her*)

Yes?

MEI LI

At that moment, that very moment, I knew I loved you.

(SHE *lowers her eyes and bows her head in humiliation and continues to speak with her head down*)

I knew I wanted to be your wife. It is necessary for me to tell you this strange thing so that you will understand how I feel now. It is because I loved you on that first day that my heart is so—hurt—today.

(SHE *raises her head and looks him in the eyes*)

I do not love you any more!

(SHE *rushes from the room.* TA *is deeply moved.* WANG *enters, senses that all is not well and gestures inquiringly to* TA)

TA

She won't marry me.

WANG

She is a foolish, willful girl.

TA

I cannot find it in my heart to agree with you. She is an unusual girl . . . I didn't know her.

WANG

She would have been a good wife.

TA

You chose well, Father. A son does not like to say so, but you are a wiser man than I.

WANG

It would be strange if a man my age were not wiser than a man your age.

TA

But in judging young women—it's been a long time since you have had to study them.

WANG

A man never stops studying young women.

TA

I have the feeling that Mei Li has just drifted past me—out of my life.

(HE *sings:*)
This is the girl whose laugh I heard,
Silver and soft and bright,
Soft as the fall of lotus leaves
Brushing the air of night.
While her flower boat
Sailed away,
Gently her eyes looked back on mine,
Clearly she heard me say:
"You are the girl I will love some day."

(DR. LI *and* MEI LI *enter carrying their luggage.*)

DR. LI

(*Addressing* WANG)
I am grateful for your hospitality, Master Wang. The time has

come for us to leave you. Please believe that our reasons are good ones.

(DR. LI *bows, crosses to door, opens it and exits.* MEI LI *follows, bows to* WANG, *approaches door, turns and takes a long look at* TA *and exits, closing door, as cutain falls.*)

END OF SCENE TWO

ACT TWO

Scene 3

SAMMY FONG'S *Penthouse Apartment*

SCENE: *It is furnished in a modern and masculine manner. Through a large window at the back are the lights of the city. Left Center, along the back wall is a bookcase with a radio on one of the shelves. There is a sofa down Center and a card table on the extreme Left of the set. A door Right leads to the hall.*

AT RISE: *A fan tan game is winding up. The players are* SAMMY, FRANKIE *and two others. Girls are kibitzing at the table or lounging about the room waiting for the game to break up.*

FRANKIE

There he goes again.

FIRST MAN

I'm cleaned out.

SECOND MAN

Me too.

FRANKIE

Look—not a smile on his face! Don't you enjoy winning a fortune?

GIRL

Sammy is carrying a torch for Linda.

SAMMY

You said it. A great big one.

FRANKIE

(*Paying up*)

I wish you'd get lucky in love again. This is the last of what I won on the Daily Double.

SAMMY

Frankie, I'm going to buy you a brocaded crying towel.

FRANKIE

Thanks.

SAMMY

What are you fellows kicking about? Look at all these beautiful flamingos you've got here—waiting to go to supper with you.

FRANKIE

Supper! Who's got any dough left to buy supper?

SAMMY

Tell you what I'll do. You all go to the Celestial Bar and sign my name to the tab. You gave the party here, I'll give it there.

(*The doorbell rings.* SAMMY *answers it admitting* MADAM FONG *and* DR. LU FONG)

SAMMY

Hello Uncle, hello Mama—

MADAM FONG

Hello, my son.

SAMMY

We just finished dinner—having our tea.

FRANKIE

Sammy cooked us a wonderful goose.

MADAM FONG

My son is a fine host. Sit down, gentlemen.

SAMMY

They were just leaving.
      (HE *gives his friends a signal to get out. They start*)

FIRST MAN

You must give us revenge, Sammy—

SAMMY

Anytime. So long, glad you liked it. We must do it again sometime.
      (THEY *have all gone*)

DR. LU FONG

You seem very happy. It must have been a wonderful dinner.

MADAM FONG

Too bad a man who can cook like Sammy should live alone.

SAMMY

I don't mind living alone, Mama, not the way I do it.
      (*The door opens and* LINDA LOW *lets herself in with
      her key.* SHE *looks at the group and stops short, embar-*

rassed. MADAM FONG *and* DR. LU FONG *exchange puzzled glances*)

LINDA

Oh, excuse me—

SAMMY FONG

(*Breaks in*)
This young lady is an employee from the Celestial Bar.

LINDA

I am here to see Mr. Fong on business.

MADAM FONG

Oh, I see.

SAMMY

My mother, why don't you and Uncle go on ahead to the Family Association. I'll meet you there.

MADAM FONG

Very well, my son—business first.
(SHE *starts out stiffly, shooting a look at* LINDA. DR. LU FONG *follows her with a knowing smile*)

DR. LU FONG

An interesting business!

SAMMY

(*After* THEY *exit*)
What's the idea of barging in here without ringing the bell?

LINDA

Why should I ring the bell when I've got a key? Here it is. I came to get my clothes.

114

SAMMY

Why?

LINDA

After what you did to me last night?

SAMMY

Listen, deep down in that plastic heart of yours you know you can't live without me, and I can't live without you.

LINDA

You go and live with your picture bride.

SAMMY

Listen, baby, you're going way back in history now. I unloaded her yesterday. I gave my contract to old Master Wang so she could marry Ta, and you could marry me.

LINDA

Who said I wanted you?

SAMMY

You said it in a thousand ways. The way you look at me, the way you kiss me, the way you fight with me. Every lump you've raised on my head has told me you're nuts about me.

LINDA

I've heard that before.

SAMMY

(Earnestly)
I'm talking marriage.

LINDA

(*Impressed*)
Marriage?

SAMMY

This time I mean it.

LINDA

You've always meant it at the time, but then something always
happened the next day.

SAMMY

This time it goes. It was written long before we were born,
baby—we were both born in the year of the horse.

LINDA

(*After a pause*)
You've horsed around too many times—

SAMMY

(*Going to phone*)
This time I'll prove it to you. Don't blow this. I'm in the money
and the mood at the same time, it may never fall that way
again.
(HE *dials*)
Hello . . . Three Family Association? This is Sammy Fong.
Who is this? Dr. Lee Chong?
(HE *bows respectfully*)
Hello doctor—when my mother gets there tell her I'm coming
over to have her meet her future daughter-in-law. Thank you,
doctor.
(HE *hangs up*)
There you are baby, we're as good as married.

LINDA

Nothing's as good as married.

(LINDA *sings:*)

Now that we're going to be married,
I'll keep imagining things,
Things that can happen to people
When they are wearing gold rings:

SAMMY

Being together each morning,
Sharing our coffee and toast—
That's only one of the pictures.
Here's what I picture most:
REFRAIN: Sunday,
          Sweet Sunday,
          With nothing to do,
          Lazy
          And lovely,
          My one day with you,
          Hazy
          And happy,
          We'll drift through the day.
          Dreaming the hours away.
          While all the funny papers lie or fly
              around the place,
          I will try my kisses on your funny
              face.
          Dozing,
          Then waking
          On Sunday, you'll see
          Only
          Me!

FLOWER DRUM SONG

(*The curtains close behind them as* LINDA *sings a* REFRAIN *to* SAMMY. *The number is then developed into an elaborate ensemble dance.*)

END OF SCENE THREE

ACT TWO

Scene 4

SCENE: *Meeting Hall of the* THREE FAMILY ASSOCIATION.
It is elaborately decorated in the Chinese manner.

AT RISE: *The Elders of the Three Family Association are
holding a session. The heads of each family,*
WANG, DR. LU FONG, *and* GEORGE CHON, *an old
wrinkled man, are center, seated in high-backed
chairs. A witness box on a small raised platform,
with elbow rest, and wooden bars, is set up Left
of center. To the left of the witness box, a bench
on which* DR. LI *and* MEI LI *are seated. Other
members of the Association are grouped around on
either side behind the Elders.* MR. POON *stands in
the witness box facing the Judges.*

WANG

Mr. Poon, you have told us that you paid your gambling debt,
because it was a debt of honor, and you have told the Ping
Wah Super-market to whistle for their money, because they
threatened to bring you to Court. It is the decision of the Family Association that the Ping Wah Super-market tear up their
bill, which will make that a debt of honor, too, since they will
only have your word you will pay it. We insist that you pay
it at once, or your restaurant will be boycotted, and you will
be dropped from the Family Association.

Next case, please!

(MR. POON *accepts the decision with a resigned bow, and
leaves.* DR. LI *steps into the witness box.*)

DR. LI

Venerable Elders of the Three Family Association. I am honored to stand before you.

(HE *reaches into his pocket and brings forth a contract, which he gives to one of the* ELDERS)

I have here a contract entered into by Madam Fong, for the marriage of her son, Sammy, to my daughter, Mei Li. My daughter is exactly as her picture represented her, and if the Elders wish to examine her they may do so.

(MEI LI *crosses to the witness box*)

DR. LU FONG

Your contract is valid, and it will be honored, Dr. Li.

(MADAM FONG *comes forward and crosses to* MEI LI *delightedly*)

MADAM FONG

At last it is you. We didn't know you were here.

(SHE *puts her arm around* MEI LI *warmly*)

My dear future daughter-in-law.

DR. LI

Your son knew we were here. Did he not tell you?

MADAM FONG

A little while ago he telephoned and said he was coming here to announce his betrothal.

DR. LU FONG

(*Smiles*)

That's Sammy, always trying to surprise us!

DR. LI

In that case, I am honored.

(HE *bows*)

MADAM FONG

I know you will be happy, Mei Li.
(MEI LI *nods sadly*)

MEI LI

Thank you, Madam Fong.

DR. LU FONG

(*To* DR. LI)
Where are you staying?

DR. LI

We have not found a hotel.

MADAM FONG

You must stay at the home of my son till the marriage.

DR. LI

You are most kind. And now, if you will permit me, I will
take my daughter out to dinner.

MADAM FONG

Nonsense, there is food here in the dining hall. George, you
will please see they have dinner.

GEORGE

Of course, Madam Fong. Come, Dr. Li.
(GEORGE *starts leading* DR. LI *and* MEI LI *upstage.* SAMMY
FONG *enters.* DR. LI *stops his daughter and* GEORGE *and
they stand upstage Left listening, unseen by* SAMMY)

SAMMY

My dear mother, honorable relatives and friends! I know that you will be happy to hear that I am finally ready to settle down and raise prize children.

(THEY *all turn and exchange looks with each other, suppressing their laughter.*)

She is a fine girl, from a distinguished family.

(THEY *laugh again.* SAMMY *looks puzzled.*)

What's the matter—don't you think I can land a girl like that?

(THEY *all nod and smile*)

Well I'm going to let you see for yourselves. You're going to meet the future Mrs. Sammy, and I know you'll all take her to your hearts and love her as I have—

(*quickly checking himself*)

as I *do!*

MADAM FONG

Stop surprising us, Sammy. She's here.

(SHE *beckons to* MEI LI *and* DR. LI)

Come, Mei Li.

(MEI LI *comes downstage and stands there.* SAMMY *stares at her stunned.*)

Welcome your bride, my son.

SAMMY

(*Not moving, but giving a sickly wave with his hand.*)

Hi.

(MEI LI, *in imitation lifts her finger in greeting*)

WANG

(*Stepping forward*)

Dr. Li, it is the custom of our Family Association, when a young man introduces his bride to the Elders for the first time, he makes a public proposal of marriage.

DR. LI

I understand, so that the Elders may bear witness.

WANG

It makes the betrothal official, and binds the young couple almost as if they were already married.

(HE *turns to* SAMMY)

Sammy!

(SAMMY *is out on his feet and doesn't answer*)

MADAM FONG

(*Very sternly*)

Sammy!

SAMMY

Yes Mama . . .

(HE *walks over to* MEI LI, *swallows hard and starts to sing to her what sounds like a proposal to the Elders, but what has special meaning for her.*)

(*Singing*)

    If you want to have a rosy future,

    And be happy as a honey bee

    With a husband who will always love you, baby—

(*Orchestra plays musical line to which he formerly sang:* "Don't marry me." SAMMY *shakes his head and hums significantly to* MEI LI)

(LINDA *enters at this point, unseen by* SAMMY)

    In the presence of my Chinese uncles,

    I'm as serious as I can be,

    I am saying this because I love you, darling—

(*Shaking his head and making a peculiar noise*)

    . . . marry me!

(*As* HE *finishes singing he turns and sees* LINDA, *and makes an even more peculiar noise!*)

MADAM FONG

(*Oblivious*)

Come, dear friends, let us drink a toast to my son and his lovely bride.

(THEY *all start off*)

SAMMY

Mama, I'll be with you in a minute.

MADAM FONG

Come now, Sammy, this is no time to talk business.

SAMMY

No, Mama, I gotta say something to her first out here.

(WANG SAN *and* SUSIE *wander onstage*)

SAMMY

(*To* LINDA)

Don't jump the gun! I was framed. Someone pulled a fast one on me.

LINDA

You are the lowest, sneakiest, slimiest—

SAMMY

Forget the superlatives, give me a chance to explain.

LINDA

Explain what? Half an hour ago you *had* to marry me, you couldn't live without me . . .

SAMMY

And nothing's changed.

LINDA

Nothing's changed! You're going to marry *her*!

SAMMY

That's the only thing that's changed.

MADAM FONG

(*Offstage*)
Sammy!

SAMMY

Coming, Mama!
(SAMMY *runs off, glad to escape from* LINDA)

SAN

(*Coming down to* LINDA)
Forget about him—why don't you wait till I grow up?

LINDA

That's a good idea, champ.

SUSIE

You're lucky to be rid of Sammy Fong.
(*The other* KIDS *enter*)

LINDA

You're right Susie—trouble with me is I don't know when I'm lucky.
(SHE *breaks into tears, and hurries off up Right*)

GIRL

What's the matter with her?

FLOWER DRUM SONG

                    SUSIE
(*Shrugs*)
She doesn't know when she's lucky.
    (*She starts to sing*)
        Well, the more I see of grown-ups,
        The less I want to grow.

                    ALL
        The more I see what they have learned
        The less I want to know.

                    SAN
        And yet we've got to all grow up—
        There's no place else to go.

                    SUSIE
        I wonder why we're all so poor
        And they've got all the dough!

                    ALL
        What are we going to do about
        The Other Generation?

                    BOY
        How will we ever communicate
        Without communication?

                    ALL
        When we are using words the modern way,

                    SAN
        They're much too big to try to dig
        The colorful things we say.

ALL

If we could take over the training of
The Other Generation
We know we could improve them quite a lot.

GIRL

But they will never let us,
They stay the way they met us,
And so we're simply stuck with what we've got—

ALL

(You can't improve them)
The kids are simply stuck with what they've got!

ALL

What are we going to do about
The Other Generation?

GIRL

How are we going to stop them when they
Start an explanation
Of "What it used to mean to be a kid!"

SAN

The clean and wholesome fun they had
The innocent things they did!

BOY

They all had a wonderful childhood in
The Other Generation.

SAN

The games they'd play were bright and gay and loud.

GIRL

They used to shout: "Red Rover,
Red Rover please come over!"

SUSIE

They must have been an awful droopy crowd
When they were younger!

ALL

They must have been an awful droopy crowd!

END OF SCENE FOUR

ACT TWO

Scene 5

SCENE: SAMMY FONG's *Penthouse Apartment.*

AT RISE: MEI LI, *wearing a kimono over her nightgown, is watching the late show on television. The set is at right angles to the audience so that the light from the screen can be seen, but not the picture.*

MALE VOICE ON TV

Ursula, come away with me! You don't belong here with him. I will make a new life for you. I love you!

FEMALE VOICE

No Carl, you mustn't kiss me. We haven't the right . . . . No Carl! . . . . OH . . . Carl.

(MEI LI *watches, enthralled. She strikes a pose, timidly imitating the woman on the screen, in the spell of a great love. The* DOORBELL *rings.* MEI LI *looks towards the door, turns off the television, runs to the door and opens it.* WANG TA *stands in the doorway, a small box in his hands)*

TA

Hello, Mei Li.

MEI LI

Hello, too, Wang Ta.

TA

May I come in?

MEI LI

This is not my home, but I can ask my father.

TA

Please don't disturb him. I just came to bring you a wedding present.
(HE *hands her a box.*)
It was my mother's clock. She wanted it to go to the girl my father selected. So, *you* really should have it.

MEI LI

(*Having opened the box*)
It is very beautiful. I will always treasure it. You must thank your father.

TA

He doesn't know I have given it to you.

MEI LI

Oh . . . thank *you*, Wang Ta.
(DR. LI *enters from Left. He wears a robe over his night-gown*)

TA

Good evening, Dr. Li. I hope I did not disturb you.

DR. LI

No, Wang Ta. Please come in.

MEI LI

(*Crossing to* DR. LI)
Wang Ta has brought a wedding present, a gift from the Wang
Chi-Yang family.
(SHE *shows him the box.* HE *takes it.*)

DR. LI

You have brought a very beautiful gift.

MEI LI

(*To* TA)
Would you like some tea?

TA

No. Please don't bother.
(DR. LI *sits down wearily in front of TV set*)

MEI LI

(*To fill in an awkward silence, she sings:*)
"Filter, Flavor, Flip-top box." . . . .
(SHE *sits on settee*)
I was watching a late show movie.

TA

Do you enjoy American movies?

MEI LI

Oh yes, in the movies every American has a beautiful auto-
mobile, and a beautiful golden girl in a car, who wears wonderful clothes. They all seem so happy, but I don't understand
why they all go around killing each other.

TA

They have to do something exciting late at night or people
would fall asleep.

MEI LI

We wait sometimes for Sammy Fong to come home—sometimes after the Late, Late, Late Show. Do we not Father?

(DR. LI *does not answer. His head hangs on his chest, and he appears to be fast asleep.*)

He's asleep. He falls asleep in front of television even when it isn't on.

TA

My aunt said you were having a Chinese wedding.

MEI LI

Yes. It is the wish of my mother-in-law.

TA

We hardly ever have real Chinese weddings over here. I've never seen one.

MEI LI

They are very nice. The bride is carried through the streets in a sedan chair to the groom's family, and when she arrives, we kneel before the Altar of Ancestral Tablets and bless them. Then we drink from a double goblet. And when the bridegroom lifts the veil, he can look on his wife's face.

TA

You have a beautiful face, Mei Li.

MEI LI

Same face.

TA

Is that all there is to the ceremony? Doesn't he even kiss the bride?

MEI LI

Why should he? They are already married.

TA

Here they are not really married till they seal it with a kiss.

MEI LI

Everything in America ends with a kiss. What does it mean?
Why do they do it?

TA

Well, it expresses what you feel and when you do it to the
right person, you light up inside as if you swallowed a swarm
of lightning bugs.

MEI LI

Why should just touching lips together do that?

TA

It does . . . it's hard to explain.

MEI LI

Maybe it would be easier if you show me.

TA

Yes, it would.

MEI LI

Then do it.
    (WANG TA *moves to a spot farther away from the sleeping
    old man*)

TA

Come here.
    (MEI LI *goes to him and holds her head up and puckers*

her lips, holding her arms out behind her like the woman on TV)
What's that for?

MEI LI

It is the kiss position I saw on the television.

TA

It isn't posed for. It's done on the inspiration of the moment. Sometimes by surprise—it's a strong personal attachment—induced by sympathetic understanding—do you understand?

MEI LI

No.

TA

Well, physically—let us say it's an action, loved by everybody in the Western countries, especially here in America.

MEI LI

What is the action?

TA

I will show you.
(MEI LI takes her stance for the kiss again)
Relax. Close your eyes, it is better if you don't stare at me.
(HE is stalling to pluck up courage)
That's right.
(HE sneaks a look to see if the old man is still asleep, then holds MEI LI with both his hands and plants a gentle kiss on her lips)

MEI LI

Can I open my eyes, now?

TA

Yes.

MEI LI

Is that the kiss which does all those things?

TA

Well, no. Compared to the kisses you see in the movies, this was only half done.

MEI LI

Only half done?

TA

Yes.

MEI LI

Do a "well done" please!
(WANG TA *takes her in his arms and holds her in a long kiss. When he lets her go, she sighs happily*)
I like it well done.

TA

So do I.

MEI LI

Your heart is beating. Can you feel mine?

TA

I love you, Mei Li.

MEI LI

(*Breaking away*)
Many times I have been sorry for what I said to you that morn-

ing. Has no one ever changed the mind of a Family Association?

TA

Never. But there is always a first time, and I'm going to try. I'm not going to sleep tonight. I'm going to walk the streets. I'm going to try to think of a way.

MEI LI

A way?

TA

To marry you.

MEI LI

All right, Ta. Do not sleep tonight. Try to think of something.

TA

I will. Goodnight, my darling.
(HE *gives her another kiss and starts for the door*)

MEI LI

Goodnight my darling too. Try to think of something.
(TA *exits.* MEI LI *crosses to her father and shakes him gently*)
My father, he has gone.

DR. LI

I did not sleep. I heard everything.

MEI LI

Oh, Father, I do not want to marry Sammy Fong. I love Wang Ta.
(DR. LI *shakes his head with finality*)

DR. LI

It is too late to talk that way. I am going to bed. Do not stay up too long, my child.

(DR. LI *exits*)

MEI LI

How can I sleep when Ta is walking the streets, trying to think of something? Oh, streets, please give him an idea!

(MEI LI *goes to TV set, and turns it on.*)

MEXICAN GIRL'S VOICE ON TV

Señor Sheriff, I must give myself up!

SHERIFF'S VOICE

Don't tell me you held up the Wells Fargo Stage at Eagle Rock!

MEXICAN GIRL'S VOICE

I came to the United States illegally across the Rio Grande—I am a *wetback!*

SHERIFF'S VOICE

You know the penalty.

MEXICAN GIRL'S VOICE

Si, Sheriff, send me back to Mexico. I cannot marry with Rodriquez. He is in love with another woman, and he is a wetback too!

END OF SCENE FIVE

ACT TWO

Scene 6

Grant Avenue

SCENE: *The drop of this shallow set attempts to convey only an impression of San Francisco's China-town. In front of it hang long, narrow, streaming banners.*

AT RISE: *Three children run on and point off Left. Then the reason for their excitement comes on, the pro-cession of a Chinese wedding. First come eight bridesmaids in flowing red gowns, then men and girls carrying elaborate candelabra, gold birdcages, articles of furniture, firecrackers and other attri-butes of a traditional Chinese wedding. Then four men carry on a sedan chair which bears the bride, dressed in red bridal costume, masked by a heavy golden veil. Following her come more of the marchers, but before they have made their exit, the drop and the banners fly away, the next scene "dissolving" through this one.*

ACT TWO

Scene 7

Ball Room of the Three Family Association.

SCENE: *The set is dominated by a very large bed on a platform, up Center.*

AT RISE: *The head of the procession is coming into the room as the rear is still leaving the previous set. Chandeliers are being lowered, wings are sliding in to form this new set. The entire company are on stage. Presently the sedan chair is carried on and lowered.* SAMMY FONG *helps* MEI LI *out of the chair and leads her in a circle around the stage in front of the guests. He is a gloomy bridegroom, going through with something he's been trapped into. They stop and kneel before the bed up Center. An attendant hands* SAMMY *the double goblet, from which he drinks. He passes it to his bride but suddenly she turns away, and dramatically tearing the veil from her face, comes downstage and faces the guests.*

MEI LI

Honorable Sirs, and my future mother-in-law, I must confess something. I came into this country illegally—across the Pacific Ocean. It is for that I cannot marry with your son. My back is wet!

MADAM FONG

You came in illegally?

MEI LI

I must give myself up. I will tell the Sheriff!

TA

(*Stepping forward*)
As a law student I can tell you that illegal entry breaks a marriage contract.

MADAM FONG

(*Anxiously*)
It does?

TA

It's at the bottom. You didn't read the small Chinese print.

SAMMY

Did you hear that, Mama?

MADAM FONG

My son cannot marry a wetback!

LINDA

Sammy! Listen to your Mama.
(SAMMY *crosses to* MADAM FONG)
No! This one!
(HE *turns and goes to* LINDA)

TA

I'll gladly marry a wetback!

140

WANG

You will do this without my consent?

TA

Yes, my father.
(HE *goes to* MEI LI)

WANG

Then I will give my consent.

TA

(*Softly, to* MEI LI)
You thought of something.

MEI LI

Ta, tomorrow we must go to the Temple of Tin How and thank the Goddess of Heaven for Television.

TA

(*Singing very softly*)
A hundred million miracles
Are happening every day

ALL

(*Coming down to footlights, all singing very softly*)
And those who say they don't agree
Are those who do not hear or see
(*Singing louder and increasing in volume until the last note*)
A hundred million miracles
Are happening every day.

CURTAIN

END OF PLAY